Horse and Pony MAGAZINE

BETTER RIDING

Jackie Budd

RINGPRESS

Ringpress Books

**PO Box 8, Lydney,
Gloucestershire,
United Kingdom
GL15 6YD**

First published 1996
in association with
Horse & Pony Magazine

© 1996 Ringpress Books Ltd.
and Jackie Budd

ISBN 1 86054 076 7

Printed and bound in
Singapore

1 2 3 4 5 6 7 8 9 10

All photographs courtesy of
Horse & Pony Magazine.

CONTENTS

WHEN you begin riding, it is important to learn to do everything as correctly as possible. That is because riding is more than just learning how to stay on board a pony and controlling him to make him go, stop and turn, or to jump over a fence.

It is all about learning to communicate with him. Never forget that ponies are a different species to us. They think quite differently and do not talk our language. Learning to ride is to do with being able to help a pony to understand what we want, and making it easy for him to do it well.

To get off to the right start you need to have a good riding teacher to explain things to you. You also need to learn on co-operative ponies that are likely to do as you ask, so long as you ask correctly. So, finding a good riding school to get you going is crucial.

Even when you think you have got the hang of riding – and perhaps have a pony of your own – the very best riders will always tell you that you never stop learning. Take regular lessons from a proper instructor to make sure no bad habits are creeping in, or to help iron out any riding problems that might arise.

TIP

Even if you ride only once a week, spend the days in between finding out all you can about horses and ponies. Learn about the different parts of the horse and its saddlery – it will come in handy for lessons. Helping at the stables is a great way of gaining experience. And never be afraid to ask questions!

Finding a good riding school

YOU or your parents may not have had much to do with horses before, but it is not hard to tell a good place to learn to ride from a bad one. Whether the school you plan to use is large or small, here are a few pointers:

■ **A friendly welcome: Well-run schools have cheerful, polite staff who are happy to help you.**

■ **A neat yard: Even if it is not all brand new, the yard and tack room should be tidy with clean, roomy stables kept in good repair. There should be plenty of pasture for the**

'Horses should look clean and alert'

The correct gear ...

For your first lessons there is no need to buy loads of expensive gear, so long as you are wearing comfy and practical clothes and get two important items – boots and a riding hat.

Hat You must wear a proper riding helmet up to the latest approved standard (in the UK this is currently labelled PAS 015, though BS4472 hats are also very safe). Some schools lend or hire hats, but it is better to buy one fitted properly just for you. If a hat does not fit well it will not give much protection – it must sit well down on the head, not tip back or forward, and be snug but not tight. The 'jockey skull' type hats *(right)* can be smartened up with a velvet or silk cover.

started

Welcome aboard: look for a well-run school with cheerful staff to help you when you are new to riding

ponies that are turned out, safe fencing and a tidy muck-heap, away from the stables.

Happy horses: Make sure the ponies look content, well-fed, clean and alert. Check their feet are in good condition and they have no sore spots.

Safety first: Riders should all be wearing up-to-date helmets. Ponies should be well-behaved and suitable for their riders. In the yard, tools should be put away and first-aid and fire equipment close to hand, with 'No Smoking' a strict rule.

Lesson time: Watch a lesson *(right)* to see if everyone seems to be having a good time and learning, too. Class lessons should have no more than six pupils.

Facilities: It helps if the school has an all-weather outdoor manege, or, better still, an indoor arena.

Boots
Any sturdy shoes or boots will do for starters, so long as they have a small heel and no buckles. Wellies are not safe, as the sole can easily get stuck in the stirrup – nor are trainers. Proper riding boots – either long rubber ones or short 'jodhpur' boots – are not too expensive.

Other kit that will make you more comfortable and safer:

Jodhpurs:
Close-fitting trousers.

Gloves:
Protect your hands.

Body protector:
A padded waistcoat that will help absorb the impact in case you fall off.

TIP

Ask local horse experts like a farrier, saddler or a Pony Club secretary if they can recommend a riding school. Approval by recognised riding organisations (like the British Horse Society or Association of British Riding Schools) will guarantee certain standards.

AT your first lesson the instructor will probably take a little while explaining some basic things to you about the pony you will be riding and the tack he is wearing. She should have chosen a pony that is the right size for you and is used to beginners, so is sensible and well-mannered.

It will all seem pretty strange at first. If you have never ridden before even the movement of the pony's walk might seem uncomfortable and fast-moving.

But don't worry – with the help of your teacher you will soon be feeling confident and in control.

LISTEN OUT FOR THE BASICS

Lunge lessons

YOU might start with a few individual lessons on the lunge. This is where the instructor stands in the middle of the arena circling the pony around her on the end of a long rein called a lunge line.

Lunge lessons help you learn quickly, because you can focus on the way you are sitting and can relax knowing that the instructor has control of where the pony is going, and how fast. Lessons on the lunge are good for all riders because they help improve your 'seat' (the way you are sitting in the saddle) and teach you to keep your balance.

YOU may be offered either private lessons or class lessons, where you will be learning in a group. Class lessons are cheaper and fun, because you have the company of others and can also learn from watching them. But at the start it is worth paying out a bit extra for a few individual lessons to get you going. Whichever you choose, the instructor will probably start off by leading you or having a helper lead you, just until you feel confident and have learnt the right signals to tell the pony what you want him to do. These signals are called the **aids**.

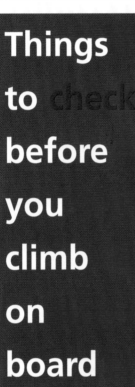

Things to check before you climb on board

MANY ponies think it's a big joke to blow their tummies out when the saddle is first put on. This means that when you come to mount, the girth (the strap which fastens the saddle on the pony) is far too loose – if you tried to get on, you would probably end up underneath rather than on top of it! So first, lift up the saddle flap and tighten both of the buckles of the girth, so the saddle will not slip around. Walk around the front of the pony and check that the buckles are level there, too. Once the girth is tight, pull each of the fore legs forwards to even out any wrinkles in the skin.

NOW pull the stirrup irons down the back of the leathers to the bottom. Standing alongside the pony, facing the saddle, check that the stirrups will be about the right length for you. Do this by clenching your fist and holding it up against the stirrup bar (where the leathers attach to the saddle). The iron should just about reach to your armpit. If no-one is holding your pony for you, always have an arm looped through the reins while you are doing these checks. Never leave the pony standing loose.

GETTING up into the saddle is called mounting, and this is one of the first things you will learn at your riding school. Mounting the right way is important for safety's sake, but also to make the whole process comfortable for the pony.

When you are first learning to mount, your instructor or a helper will probably hold the pony to make sure he stands still. If you are getting on from the ground, it is also helpful to have someone pulling down on the stirrup iron on the far side of the saddle to stop the saddle moving around on the pony's back as you get on.

More experienced riders can practise mounting from either side of the pony, but usually a pony is mounted from his near (left-hand) side.

How to get on board . . .

Step by Step

1 **STAND on the pony's near side with your left shoulder alongside his shoulder, facing towards his tail. Gather up the reins so they are quite short but not tight, to stop the pony moving off. Putting both reins into the left hand, place your hand on the pony's mane just above the withers. The spare ends of the reins need to be dropped over the other side of the pony's neck out of the way. If you have a whip, hold it in your left hand, so it doesn't wave about.**

2 **TAKE the stirrup iron in your right hand, bringing the far side towards you – this will make sure the leather lies flat under your leg once you are on. Keeping your weight forward, put your left foot well into the stirrup, so the ball of the foot is well on to the iron. Now hop round so you are facing the pony's side, pressing down into the stirrup as much as you can so your toe goes under the belly instead of poking into it. Your right hand goes either on the pony's withers, perhaps grasping a bit of mane, on the pommel (front) of the saddle or, if you can reach, over the far side of the saddle at the waist (middle section). Never hang on to the cantle (back), as this can twist and damage the saddle.**

hints

...and how not to do it!

3 NOW push up with your right foot with as much spring as you can. Straighten your left knee so you are standing in the stirrup and swing your right leg well clear over the pony's back. Your right hand now needs to move to the pommel of the saddle.

WHOOPS! You can tell by the expression on his face (above) what this pony thinks of having his rider's toe digging him in the ribs as she gets on. Keep your toe down as you pivot round. Your pony could easily mistake a nudge in the side as a signal to walk on – the last thing you want when you're trying to mount!

OUCH! Dragging your right leg across the pony's quarters (below) is a sure way to make him jump forwards in surprise. Lift your leg well clear – and gather up those reins too!

4 AS your leg swings over, turn your body to face forwards and lower yourself gently into the saddle. Do not come down with a thump! Without letting go of the reins, see if you can feel for the other stirrup and put your right foot in – at first you may need to look down and check where it is and that the leather is not twisted. Now you can take up the reins in both hands. With just one or two adjustments you are ready to go.

HAVING A LEG-UP

THIS is especially useful for a small person getting on a big horse! You gather up the reins in your left hand and stand facing the pony's near side. Put your right hand over the saddle. Now bend your left knee up so your helper can hold it. Count:

"One, two..." and on the "three" your helper pushes you up at the same time as you spring off your right foot. As you go up, swing your leg well clear over the pony's back and land lightly in the saddle. It is better to hold the far side of the saddle rather than the cantle, as shown here.

VAULTING ON

THIS is for the real experts (on small ponies!) With your left hand holding the reins on the withers and your right hand reaching over the seat of the saddle, bend your knees and spring up. You need to push down on your arms until your body is well over the pony's back, high enough to swing your leg clear over the saddle.

USING A MOUNTING BLOCK (above)

THIS is handy if the saddle is a long way up! It also puts less strain on the pony's back than the ordinary way of mounting, so if your yard has a mounting block it's worth using it. Position the pony alongside the block so it is next to the saddle. Gathering up the reins in your left hand and standing on the block, put your left foot in the stirrup. With your right hand over the saddle, get on and settle down lightly.

hints 2

Essential checks after mounting

WHOA! Before you can move off, there are just a couple more checks to make to be sure the saddle is secured in the correct position and your stirrups are fixed at the right length for your legs. If you have ever ridden in a slipping saddle you will know how dangerous this can be. And stirrups that are too long or short mean you will not be able to balance properly or use your legs very effectively. So it is important to get these things right to start with.

ADJUSTING THE STIRRUPS

TAKE your feet out of the stirrups and let them hang loose. As a rough guide, the bottom of the iron should be just about the same level as your ankle if the stirrups are at a suitable length. If they are too long or short, you will need to put the reins into one hand. With your foot in the iron, move your thigh back a bit, find the stirrup leather buckle under the skirt of the saddle.

Pull the buckle up, move the prong to the right hole, then pull down on the inside of the leather so the buckle slots back into place at the top. At first you will probably find you need your instructor's help. But with practice you'll soon get the hang of doing this without even looking down!

TIGHTENING THE GIRTH

SETTLE down into the saddle. If no one is holding your pony, make sure your reins are short enough to stop him moving off. Now take both reins into your right hand, laying the left one flat against the right one across your palm. Without taking your foot out of the stirrup, bring your left leg forward past the front knee roll of the saddle.

With your free hand, lift the saddle flap so you can see the girth strap. Look down, and, holding the end of the straps firmly, pull up each one in turn and tighten it as much as you can. When the buckles are in place, put down the flap and slide your leg back in place.

TIP Whichever way you choose to get on, always make sure your pony stands still until you have made all your adjustments. Letting him wander off before you are ready is a sloppy habit.

GETTING off the pony is called 'dismounting' and, as always, there is a right and wrong way to do it. When you start riding, dismounting from even a small pony seems a long way down, but before long you will be leaping off all sizes of horse and pony without ending up in a heap on the ground!

Dismounting

MAKE sure your pony is standing still. Take both feet out of the stirrups and hold both reins in your left hand. If you are carrying a whip, make sure this is also in your left hand, or it might wave about as you dismount. Put your right hand on the front of the saddle and lean well forwards.

The right way to dismount

Swing your right leg clear of the pony's back and drop down as lightly as you can, bending your knees slightly as you reach the ground. You need to finish up next to your pony's shoulder on his near (left) side. Never try to dismount by flinging your leg over the pony's withers in front of you. Dropping the reins will mean you have no control, and if your pony is frightened by seeing your leg swing up out of the corner of his eye, and moves forward, you could fall off backwards on to your head – ouch!

hints

TIP

RIDERS in some countries like the USA and Australia are taught to dismount leaving their left foot in the stirrup and stepping down. Take care not to poke your toe into the pony's side as you swing around or he might move off unexpectedly.

Step by Step

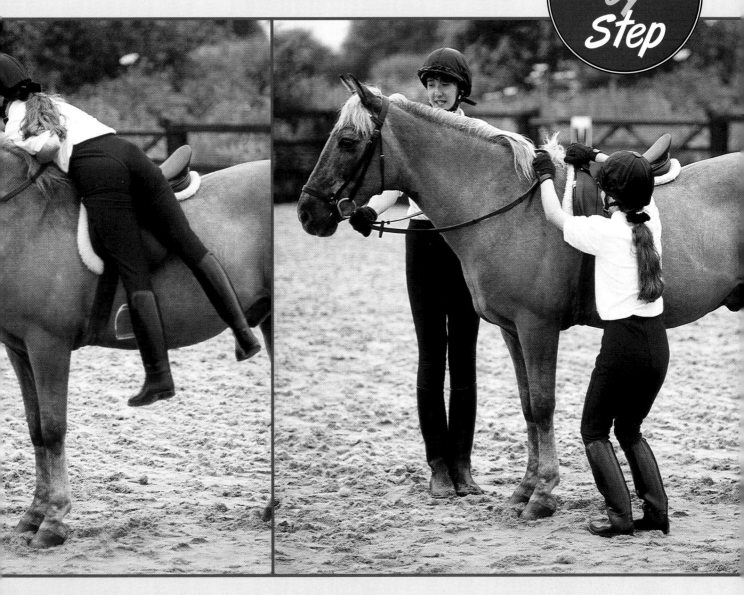

AFTER you have dismounted there are a few things to do to make your pony safe and comfortable.

RUN UP THE STIRRUPS:

THIS stops the stirrups from banging against the pony's sides and catching on something as you lead him. Take each stirrup iron and push it up the back of the leather right to the top near the buckle. Tuck the end of the leather through the iron.

LOOSENING THE GIRTH

ALLOW your pony to breathe out and relax after all his hard work by loosening off his girth a little. Once the stirrups have been run up, lift up the near-side saddle flap and release the girth strap just one or two holes. If your pony is wearing a bridle with a drop-type noseband (one that fits below the bit), it is kind to loosen this slightly after work as well.

THE reins are one method the rider has of communicating with the pony – or giving the signals known as the 'aids'. Working together with aids from your legs, the reins can be used to help ask the pony to slow down, to 'gather him up' so he moves more briskly instead of slopping along, and to turn or bend his body to one side or the other.

As soon as you mount, quickly take up the reins and adjust their length so you have control. There is a particular way to hold the reins and position your hands which means you can give your rein aids really easily and make your pony understand the slightest signal.

Holding the reins

THE rein comes from the bit and passes between your little and third fingers, goes up through your palm and comes out between your first finger and your thumb, which holds it firm.

Adjusting the reins

HOLD the rein buckle in your left hand and take up the right rein further down nearer the bit with your right hand. Hold it correctly (as above). Use your right thumb and forefinger to take hold of the left rein, freeing your left hand. Now take the left rein into the left hand properly at the same length as the other side. If you want to shorten the length of both reins, do this, one at a time, by using the opposite hand to draw the rein through each hand in turn. Shorten the reins in this way whenever you feel they are getting a bit long. You do not need to halt – you can do it as you are going along. The reins should always be the same length and never be twisted.

Where the hands go

Whenever you are riding, whatever speed you are going at, your hands must stay level with each other just above the pony's withers about 4 inches (10cm) apart. If you keep knocking your hands on the front of the saddle, or get greasy gloves or knuckles from the pony's coat, your hands are too low!

the reins

Bad hand positions

WHEN you are holding the reins the correct way, you can signal down them just by squeezing your fingers, hardly moving your hand itself at all. There should be no need to pull or tug with a backwards movement. But you must keep your thumbs on top all the time – then they can keep a grip on the rein while your other fingers do the squeezing. This way your whole hand and wrist stays relaxed and you can have a sensitive feel on the pony's mouth.

If you turn your wrists over so the knuckles are on top or your wrists are bent in (above), you lose that direct line to the pony's mouth and your whole wrist goes stiff. The same goes for sticking your thumbs right out so your palms are upwards. Always keep your thumbnails on top!

It takes quite a while to learn to keep your hands steady all the time. At first you will probably find your instructor is forever reminding you.

Keep them level

TRY not to have one hand higher than the other– your pony will get different messages from each one. Never let them cross over the pony's neck – keep them either side of the withers, even when you are turning a corner.

Contact: The 'feel' down the reins...

YOU will hear your instructor talking about having the right 'contact' with the reins. This means the 'feel' or pressure that you have on the pony's mouth.

One thing the reins are never used for is to hang on or get your balance. Ponies' mouths are very sensitive, so never be rough with the reins or jab on them to tell a pony off. However, you do need to have a feel of the pony's mouth or you won't be able to tell him what to do. It is no use going along with reins like washing lines, or the pony will be wondering what is going on. So there is no point having your reins too long or loose. But you do not want them too short and tight either, or he will be uncomfortable. Getting and keeping the correct pressure on the reins might take a while to get used to. Once you have got a good contact, try to keep that feel all the time – even if the pony's head position changes – by moving both hands slightly back or forwards.

Sitting right

HANGING on by the reins is not the way to stay on that pony, and neither is gripping as tightly as you can with your legs. Your aim is to stay up there simply by sitting upright, completely in balance, on the pony's back. So that means sitting in the right position and keeping in it, whatever the pony is doing underneath you!

The right position does more than just keep you on board and in balance. It keeps your legs and hands in exactly the right place to give the aids and send clear messages to your pony. It might feel awkward at first, so you have to concentrate hard to stay there. But as you get better and better you will find you can keep your position without thinking about it – a bit like riding a bike.

TIP

RELAX! It is really important you stay relaxed all the time when you are in the saddle. If you go all stiff you will not be able to give the aids properly, and your pony will sense straight away that you are uptight and get worried himself. So, don't try too hard and end up getting tense. Take a few deep breaths and try to sit as naturally (but not sloppily) as you can.

KEEP your head up and look between the pony's ears (inset, top). Do not look sideways or down. Try to sit up straight, without tensing your shoulders. Think about keeping your shoulders level, not dipping one down to the side. Hold your hands level just above the withers. You are aiming for a straight line from the bit, along the reins, through your wrists to your elbows.

The correct position

SIT right down deep in the very centre of the saddle. Try not to lean to one side or you will not be in balance. Sit squarely with your weight evenly spread over both of your seat-bones.

... and how not to do it!

THIS rider is sitting too stiffly, with a hollow back and tense body. She needs to bring her hands down and elbows back to get a softer contact with the pony's mouth. To give her pony a leg aid she will have to swing her whole leg back – with toes stuck out like that, she is sure to bang her heels into the pony's sides and give him a nasty shock!

LET your legs hang loosely down over the saddle flaps. Your foot is positioned with the stirrup alongside the girth, so the knee and toe are in line. The ball of the foot is on the stirrup iron, with a little weight in the iron so the toes are slightly up and the heel slightly down. The toes must point straight ahead. You should be able to draw an imaginary line through the head, shoulders, elbows and hips right down to your heels. Your instructor will help adjust your position until you know what 'feels right'.

A T last we are about to get moving! It is time to learn the aids – the instructions you use to tell the pony what you want him to do. Expert riders can give many different variations on the aids to ask a well-trained horse or pony to do quite complicated movements. But, for now, all you need to know is how to tell the pony to move forward, to slow down or stop and to make simple turns. To do this you use a combination of signals from your legs and hands. The other 'natural' aids are the voice and seat.

The aids and their uses . . .

LEGS

Your legs ask the pony to move forwards faster. They also help to keep him straight or to turn him.

HANDS

Your hands, on the reins, help to control your pony's speed and the direction he is going.

VOICE

Your voice can be useful at times to help encourage a pony, soothe him or praise him. But don't over-do it or keep chatting to your pony constantly.

SEAT

Advanced riders, who are very secure in the saddle, can use their back and seat muscles, together with their leg aids, to help balance the horse and make him move more actively. This is something you will learn about as your riding improves. For now, just concentrate on staying in a good position in the saddle. But always remember that any change in your body position shifts your weight about on the pony and will affect his balance.

Steady as you go

O NCE your pony is going forwards at the speed you want, hold your legs still, as relaxed as you can, close to his sides just behind the girth. As the pony walks, think about keeping that great position you had when he was standing still. As you feel the pony's head move forwards and back a little as he walks, you should allow your hands to follow that movement.

■ KEEP the contact on the reins steady – just ease them back and forwards, don't jerk them.

■ TRY to sit up straight with your shoulders back. Keep the top half of your body as still as you can.

■ DON'T grip on with your lower legs, just let them hang loosely down close to the pony's sides. Once you are moving, keep them still.

ARTIFICIAL AIDS

Y OU may find it useful to carry a whip, which is known as an 'artificial' aid, just to back up your legs in case your pony does not respond to them. The whip is usually carried in the hand nearest the centre of the arena (the inside hand). It fits through the palm and lies across the thigh, not down the pony's shoulder or waving about in the air!

move

Transitions

YOU will need to use the aids whenever you want to make a transition – that is, to change the pace, or speed, your pony is moving at. When you ask your pony to go up a pace, this is called an 'upward' transition. Asking him to move into a slower pace is called a 'downward' transition. Whether you are increasing speed or decreasing it, the aids to go faster are always the same and the aids to go slower are the same.

The difficult part is to stay in position and give the aids consistently, so that your pony understands them!

From halt to walk

GET your pony's attention by checking your contact is short enough and sitting up straight with your bottom well down in the saddle. Now close the lower part of your legs around the pony's sides just behind the girth.

As you give the signal, keep your heels down in the stirrups, like in the top picture, moving

your legs inwards and only slightly back.

If you kick upwards like the picture, bottom, your leg tenses up and your body has to tip forwards throwing you and the pony off balance. The aim is to be able to give each aid without having to move any other part of your body.

As the pony starts to move forwards, let your hands release the contact a little by easing slightly forwards. Now the pony knows he is

supposed to be moving on, so you can stop the leg aid. If you get your aids right and your pony is well trained, he should respond straight away. If he does not maybe he didn't 'hear' you, so check your position and try again a bit more firmly and he should respond. You will soon learn to judge how much pressure you need.

As you get better at giving the aids, in time they will be almost invisible to anyone watching!

Walking

NOW you are sitting correctly in the saddle it is time to think about walking on. This sounds simple enough – after all the pony is doing all the work! However it is important that you also play your part. Your pony must walk on actively and with energy, and you must steer him the way you want to go. Can you feel the four-time beat of the walk? It goes: one – two – three – four. Aim to get your pony walking on in a straight line, with a regular beat.

Three ways not to do it

COME on, don't let him go to sleep! If your pony won't walk on, or is dragging his feet, check your reins are short enough and use your legs again to hurry him up!

HINTS ON SLOWING DOWN

Bᴇғᴏʀᴇ we start moving any faster, we had better get to grips with how to use the pony's brakes and steering.

Walk to halt

Wʜᴇɴ you want to slow down or halt, sit as upright as you can and press your bottom down into the saddle. Keep your legs close to the pony's sides.

With a responsive pony there should be no need to pull on the reins. All you have to do is to keep your hands still, so the pony feels a resistance and knows you want to go slower. Some ponies may need just a squeeze on the reins before they get the message, but never tug or haul back on them. As soon as your pony responds, ease the pressure off so he knows he has done what you wanted.

Nᴏᴡ, would you pay any attention to a rider like this, above? Try to keep your lower leg underneath you, and close to the pony's sides. To give a leg aid, this rider will have to move her whole leg backwards. Look how her leg position has shifted all her weight to the back of the saddle so she is completely out of balance.

Yᴏᴜ can see what this pony reckons to that flapping going on behind in the picture on the right.

AS long as you are sitting squarely and centrally in the saddle and you are using both of your legs at the same place on each side of your pony, he should go straight. When you want to make a turn, each leg and each hand has a different job to do.

Your **inside** hand (that's the one towards the inside of the arena, on the side you are turning) squeezes the rein gently, making the pony turn his head and neck slightly that way to guide him round the way you want to turn.

Your **outside** hand (the one on the outside of the school or turn) is allowed to move forward slightly as the pony begins to turn his head. Both hands stay level and keep an even contact on the reins throughout the turn.

Do not release the outside hand too much, though, or the pony's head will bend too much into the turn and he might go on too fast. Use this hand to control the pony's speed, too. Your **inside** leg is pressing inwards into the pony's side, by the girth. This tells the pony to keep moving forwards. Think of the turn as bending the pony's body around this leg.

Your **outside** leg is the one that is helping the pony to turn. Use it just behind the girth to stop the pony's quarters from swinging out and to keep his body bending around the curve.

urns

Do's and Don'ts

DO turn your head slightly to look in the direction you are going. This really helps, as it turns your shoulders and hips a little that way too, so these stay in line with the pony's shoulders during the turn. The tiny change in your balance helps your pony bend through the turn. But don't strain to look – stay sitting up straight.

DO think about your turn in plenty of time so you don't take your pony by surprise. Try to make your turn a nice, even bend, not a sharp corner that throws you all out of balance.

DON'T let your pony grind to a halt! Keep him moving forwards in an active, even rhythm throughout the turn.

DON'T lean inwards (above, right), drop your inside shoulder down or slide your bottom out. Sit as upright and square as you can.

DON'T pull your pony round with the rein only, (above, left) or use too much rein and hardly any leg. You may end up turning his head and neck, but the rest of him will keep going straight! Aim to get his whole body bending in the direction you are turning. To do this you actually need hardly any pressure – just a combination of 'feel' on the inside rein, 'give' on the outside rein and 'feel' with the outside leg.

WALK is a steady pace that you will soon get the hang of. Moving up a gear to trot could take a little longer to get used to. You will probably feel that you are going quite a lot faster, and, at first, be prepared for a bumpy ride until you've mastered the skill of 'rising' to the trot. Trot is much bouncier than walk because, in trot, the pony moves in a one-two rhythm, springing from one diagonal pair of feet to the other diagonal pair, with a brief moment in between each spring when all his feet are off the ground.

Rising trot

WHEN you begin riding you will be taught 'rising trot' – which means learning to lift your seat a little out of the saddle with the trot's 'up' beat and sitting gently back in the saddle for the 'down' beat. This makes things easier on the pony's back and on your bottom!

Rising to the trot takes practice, so don't expect to grasp it straight away. Have a go in halt first, concentrating on keeping your legs in the right place, body upright and hands still while your body moves slightly up and down. The first time your pony trots you will probably tense up and tip forward and have to grab at something (make this the mane or neckstrap, not the reins!). But try to relax and keep your head and body up. Count the one-two rhythm out loud.

Let yourself be pushed up by the up-beat, your body coming slightly forwards, then back down into the saddle with the down-beat.

Concentrate on letting your weight sink down through your heels. Keep at it and, all of a sudden, you will click into time with the movement, and away you go!

TIP

Lots of riders try too hard with their rising trot(see right), standing up in the stirrups so they have got a long way to come down again with each beat. Try to relax and just let the swinging movement of the trot lift you a little way up out of the saddle. Think of just pushing your hips forward with each beat.

basics

TIP

What if you are on old lazy-bones again? Having to keep kicking him to keep him moving on in trot is throwing you right out of position when you are trying to do rising trot as well. First, check you have your reins short enough and you are not tipping forwards. Now use your whip to give him a smart smack behind the girth to encourage him to make a bit more effort. Do this immediately whenever you feel him 'switching off'.

From walk to trot

THE aids for moving from walk into trot are exactly the same as halt to walk, except that you may have to use them more firmly. First make sure your pony is awake and walking on with a spring in his step. Check your reins have a good contact.

Now sit up, press your bottom down into the saddle and squeeze (or nudge inwards, if necessary) with both legs on the pony's sides. Remember that as you ask with your legs, you have to 'allow' a little with your hands so he knows it's OK to move onwards.

Once the pony is trotting, don't start rising immediately. Sit for a few trot beats to help your balance until he is going in a good rhythm. You don't need to keep using your leg aids once the pony is trotting. Only use them again if you feel him slowing down, or want to trot on faster.

WHENEVER you want your pony to move up a pace, you must sit up as straight as you can, keep your reins short and your legs in the right place. Otherwise he does not know what is going on back there.

Trotting

Whoops!

1 NO prizes for guessing what is going wrong here (pic 1). Hands stuck out, legs forwards miles from the pony's sides, weight thumping about on the back of the saddle. No wonder this pony is not enjoying himself.

2 DON'T panic! This rider (pic 2) has got in a fluster and everything is going wrong. She's hanging on to the reins and gripping as hard as she can with her knees, so her heels have come up, throwing her forwards. Her pony thinks her legs are saying 'Go!', and is worried and confused about why she is pulling on his mouth. She needs to slow down to walk, get organised and try again – shortening the stirrups a bit will help her keep a better position.

3 CAN you see how, by falling forwards, (pic 3), the reins have got too long, the rider's legs have moved too far back and all the pony's weight has been thrown on to his front end? She would have a lot more success by sitting up in balance, shortening her reins and driving him on so his hindquarters produce more active steps.

It's all in the balance!

REMEMBER that whatever pace your pony is moving at, you are trying to keep that brilliantly balanced position you were in when he was standing still – despite all this bouncing up and down! Although your body inclines forward a bit as you rise to the trot, it should not tip your weight on to the pony's front end.

KEEP looking up between the pony's ears all the time. Your hands should be level, but unlike in walk when they 'give' with the pony's head movement, in trot they stay still. Your legs need to keep still too, even though you are rising up and down. They must stay snugly closed around the pony's sides without gripping (don't let that heel creep up!), or shooting backwards and forwards as you rise and fall.

From trot to walk

TO slow down from trot to walk, first stop rising for a few beats. Sitting as tall as you can and keeping your lower leg underneath you, closed around the pony's sides, brace your back, press your bottom down into the saddle and gently put pressure on the reins. Don't pull on the reins unless your pony takes no notice. As he eases into walk, release the pressure and allow your hands to move with his head. These riders are having trouble coming down to walk because they are tense and have forgotten to sit upright. The one on the left has tipped forward so she is looking down and her bottom is out of the saddle. Her hands are pulling and set too low. Her leg is gripping with the knee and heel, giving her horse all the wrong signals! She needs to relax and sit tall. The rider on the right is trying to slow down by hauling on the reins. Because her leg has slipped back, her pony thinks he is supposed to be going faster. She needs to loosen her shoulders, push her heels down, then relax her arms and use on-off, give-and-take squeezes on the rein to ask the pony to steady up.

Sitting trot

Trotting:

IT is possible not to rise to the trot but to stay sitting in the saddle all the time. You will see expert riders using sitting trot a lot, because when you can do it well it gives you much more control over the horse and his balance.

To sit to the trot without ending up being thrown about, you have to keep upright and stay very relaxed in your body and legs so that all the bounce is absorbed by your supple knees and hips. Sounds hard? Well, it does take a bit of practice and it is tiring at first. But as long as you don't tip forwards or grip up with your legs, you will find that staying in position by just using your balance is not as difficult as you would expect. This is what you are aiming for in all your riding – to be able to stay in balance with your pony all the time whatever he is

doing. So practising sitting trot is a great way of helping you to develop what is called an 'independent' seat – that is, to sit deep and square in the saddle and stay there without relying on the reins or stirrups. It is worth sticking at improving your sitting trot – don't forget, you actually need to sit for a few beats when you prepare to make a transition in or out of trot, and it will be especially useful when you canter. The better you are sitting, the better your transitions will be.

Ugh – no stirrups

YES, this is why your instructor is so keen on getting you riding without stirrups – because there is no better way of helping you learn to balance yourself. Of course, sitting trot without stirrups is incredibly bumpy. So, do you remember what you need to do to stay on board and even keep smiling? Sit up, look up, legs long and relax! If you do feel yourself tipping to one side, don't snatch on the reins. Grab some mane or the neckstrap, and think: 'Shoulders back, legs underneath' to get yourself upright again. Don't worry

IF YOU are asked to "Quit and cross your stirrups" in a lesson, take your feet out of both irons. (Pic 1) Pull the buckle down a little way from the stirrup bar so it does not dig into your thigh. Now take the right leather over the front of the saddle first, then the left. That is so that if you get off and want to mount again, the near-side stirrup is easy to take back.

WHEN you get going in trot, you need to learn about 'diagonals'. As we said, when a pony trots he springs from one pair of legs to the other and in rising trot the rider rises and falls to this beat.

As you start doing different exercises and movements in an arena, it becomes more important to sit and rise to the correct beat for two reasons:

■ IF you were to always rise to one particular pair of legs and sit to the other, the pony would soon become stiff and one-sided.

■ WHEN you are moving around a circle, the pony will be better balanced if you sit as his outside shoulder moves backwards. So, if you

Diagonal thinking

are going round to the right (on the right rein), you sit as the left shoulder comes back – this is the pony's left diagonal. Going around on the left rein, you sit as the right shoulder comes back – the pony's right diagonal. Experienced riders learn to tell which diagonal they are sitting on just by feel, but at first you'll need to glance down (don't lean right over) to see which shoulder is moving back as you sit.

Making a change

YOU will have to change diagonal every time you change direction, so that you always stay on the correct (outside) one.

It's simple – all you do is sit down for an extra beat. So instead of going 'up-down-up-down', you go 'up-down-down-up'. Glance down now and you will see you have changed diagonal.

The rider pictured above is going around on the right rein and is on the 'down' beat of the trot. Is she is on the correct diagonal? (Answer below).

though, your instructor should not ask you to trot without stirrups until you have got quite good at trotting with them.

Although this rider in picture 3 is leaning back a little, her legs are hanging down loose and she looks much more secure than the other one in picture 2.

Most riders have their first go without stirrups on the lunge like this, so they don't have to worry about controlling the pony.

ANSWER: No, she should be sitting as the outside shoulder comes back, not the inside one.

I T'S one thing having control over your pony when you are riding on your own or in an individual lesson. But when you join a group of other riders you will really need to have your wits about you. There is not only your riding style and your own pony to think about – you will have to watch where everyone else is going and make sure you don't get in their way!

M OST group lessons take place in an enclosed arena or indoor school. In a group like this, you will need to learn certain instructions and terms the instructor will use to keep all the riders organised. There are also some safety rules designed to avoid collisions or unnecessary accidents.

Y OU could find the quiet pony you have been used to is quite a different character when he gets with all his mates. Most ponies are livelier in a group lesson, and may try to catch you out by cutting corners, trying to drift towards the others, being reluctant to leave their friends to work on their own, or put on an extra burst of speed to catch up with the rest of the ride!

B E prepared for your pony to shy if another one comes close up behind or next to him, and always think and look ahead. Be considerate and aware of other riders.

Lesson language

TIP

Listen to what your instructor says about you, and, when you have a chance, watch the others, too. You can learn a lot from all the instructor's comments. And don't be afraid to ask questions if there is anything you are not 100 per cent sure about.

RIDE: Name for the group of riders. In most lessons the ride will follow in a single file.

LEADING FILE: The rider at the front of the line. Usually this is an energetic, forward-moving pony.

REAR FILE: The rider at the back of the line. Usually the slowest moving pony.

LEFT REIN: Going around to the left.

RIGHT REIN: Going around to the right.

CHANGE THE REIN: Moving across the arena and turning the other way when you reach the other side, so you are going the opposite way around the school.

TRACK: The path around the outside of the arena.

INSIDE TRACK: A path around the arena, 3m from the outside track.

CENTRE LINE: An imaginary line right down the centre of the school lengthways.

"PREPARE TO..." Don't worry, your instructor will always warn you when she is about to tell you to move up a pace or slow down to prepare for the transition.

GO LARGE: A command telling you to stop doing the previous movement and to carry on around the outside track.

OPEN ORDER: You can ride wherever you like in the arena, not in a line behind the other ponies. Be careful when passing other ponies if you are riding in 'open order'.

Keep to the school rules

KEEP YOUR DISTANCE

When you are riding in single file, don't let your pony go along with his nose right up to the tail of the pony in front. This is asking to get kicked. Keep a distance of at least one pony's length between you and the rider in front. If you are lagging behind, hurry your pony along to close up the gap. If your pony's pace is faster than the one ahead, it is OK to circle away and join in somewhere else, so long as you look and plan where you are going.

SLOWING DOWN AND STOPPING

Before slowing down, think first in case there is anyone right behind you, or you may cause a pile-up! If you want to go down a pace from the rest of the ride, move over on to the inside track out of their way. Go right into the centre of the school if you need to adjust your girth or stirrups (picture, right).

PASSING

Whenever you pass another rider, don't zoom by too close. Allow at least a pony's width between you. If you are travelling in opposite directions, keep a look-out for other riders approaching and always pass right hand to right hand.

The arena

MOST arenas have markers around the outside with the letters A, K, E, H, C, M, B and F. Try to learn these, because your instructor will use them when she gives commands so you know where you have to do something different. There is a way to remember the letters and their order, clockwise around the arena. They read 'All King Edward's Horses Can Manage Big Fences'! One extra letter is imaginary – X is right in the very centre of the arena.

ASK FIRST

Whenever you are coming into or leaving a school where riders are working, ask your instructor first and check to see the way is clear.

DURING your lesson the instructor will ask either the whole ride, or each rider individually in turn, to do 'school movements' or exercises. These include various turns, circles and loops which help you practise your riding skills. As you become a better rider, you can also use these exercises to help your pony become more supple and obedient – this is known as 'schooling' your pony. Listen carefully to your instructor, because she will tell you at which marker you should start and finish each movement. Here are some of the movements you are likely to come across, and what you should be aiming to achieve:

LARGE 920m CIRCLES	HALF 20m CIRCLES	SMALL CIRCLES

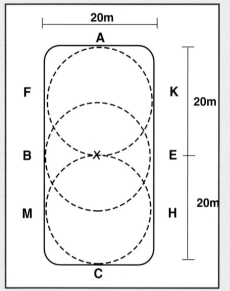

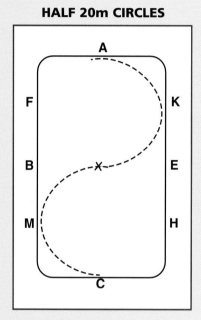

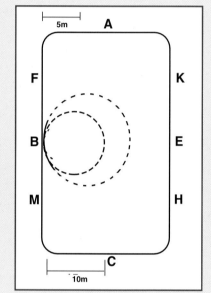

Circles

Where you go: A 'large' or '20-metre' circle takes up all of one end of the arena, touching each side and X in the centre. (diagram, above left). You could also start a large circle at B or E. Smaller circles are 10 or 15m across (diagram, right). A 10-metre circle reaches to the centre line. You may also be asked to do a half-circle, changing the rein when you get halfway round so the movement forms an 'S' shape. (diagram, centre).

Your aim: To make an even-shaped, accurate circle. To get your pony's whole body bending around the circle by using your hand and leg aids as if you were making a slight turn to the inside.

Figure of eight

Where you go: Leave the track just after a corner marker. Head diagonally across the school, passing through X – this is called going 'across the diagonal'. Carry on around the end of the school, then at the corner marker start across the diagonal again to the far side corner marker where you started. Now 'Go large'.

Your aim: To make your pony leave the track when he is asked. To keep him straight across the diagonal and reach the marker at the other side, spot-on. To make a nice bend around the short end of the school, then do the same going the other way. It should all be done in one flowing movement with no sharp corners or changes of speed.

movements

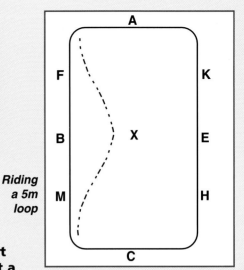

Riding a 5m loop

Serpentine

Where you go: This is a snake-shaped figure (diagram, below). For a three-loop serpentine, begin a circle at A or C. Half-way round, instead of carrying on, head across the school and begin another half-circle on the other rein. Again, half-way round, straighten up for a few paces before beginning a third half-circle the other way. You finish at the opposite end of the school to where you began. But heading the same way as you were before.

Your aim: To stay organised so you make three even loops, all touching the sides of the school. Keep your pony bending to the inside' of each half-circle, but straightening him across the centre.

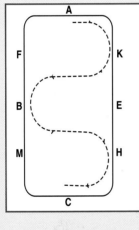

Loops

Where you go: Start leaving the track at a corner marker. Incline towards the centre line. When you are opposite B or E, start heading back to the track again. A 10-metre loop would, at its deepest point, take you to the centre line. A 5m loop is half as deep (diagram, above).

Your aim: To make your loop one flowing movement that keeps accurately to the markers, and prepare your pony for each change in 'bend' and get him bending his body through the curves.

Changing the rein

During the lesson the instructor will often ask for a 'change of rein' or direction. There are set ways of changing the rein which make it an easy movement – you don't just stop, about turn and set off in the opposite direction! The first ways you will learn are:

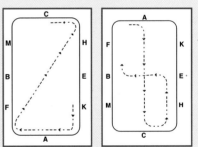

1. Turning across the diagonal (diagram, left).
2. Turning down the centre line, or
3. Turning across the centre line (both in diagram, right).

After changing the rein, always check:
● Are you on the correct diagonal? In trot, when you change direction you must remember to sit to an extra beat so you end up still on the correct (outside) diagonal after the change.
● Have you swopped your whip over? If you are carrying a whip, as a general rule you should always have it in your 'inside' hand. Then you can use it behind your inside' leg when necessary, to encourage your pony on.

At the end of the lesson, don't forget to thank your pony straight away with a pat and a few kind words. This is called 'making much of' your pony.

THERE are all sorts of exercises that can be done on board your pony that will help improve your riding, making you feel more confident and 'at home' in the saddle. Usually these are done in halt, though if you have a lunge lesson you may find your instructor asks you to do some of them on the move as your balance gets better.

Exercises like this are great fun, but you must always have someone holding the pony. Many of them involve letting go of the reins, and you would not want your pony to walk forwards unexpectedly and tip you off.

You will find that doing this kind of exercise regularly also improves your suppleness and gets your riding muscles into shape, so you don't finish every lesson feeling stiff as a board and walking like a cowboy! You will really notice the difference when you can sit deeper in the saddle, are more relaxed about your riding and can really help your pony to go well instead of getting all tense and gripping to stay on – which is what makes you stiff later.

Before you begin, you may need to quit and cross your stirrups in front of the saddle and tie a loose knot in your reins to stop them drooping down.

Round the world

First swing one leg clear of your pony's neck so you are sitting sideways. Now shuffle your bottom round and swing your leg over his rump so you are facing backwards. Next, bring your other leg over, so you are facing sideways the other way. Finish by swinging your leg back over the neck. Move your legs carefully so you don't startle your pony or lose your balance and slip off.

Arm stretching

Great for getting you sitting deep and tall in the saddle. Hang your legs down low and reach right up for the sky.

Arm circling

Do this backwards or forwards, swinging your arms round in large circles. Not too fast! Keep the legs hanging down loosely, and don't tip forward.

Arm folding

Can you fold your arms behind your back? This will really help loosen up your shoulders and make you sit tall when you are riding.

Ankle circling

Relax those legs. Now circle your ankles around slowly, first clockwise and then anti-clockwise. This will help you keep your heels down and toes forwards when you take your stirrups back – without even thinking about it!

exercises

Trunk twisting

Arms straight out at shoulder height. No drooping! Now swing them slowly from side to side. Try and keep your hips in line with your pony's shoulders at all times, so you are really suppling up your waist.

Toe touching

Another great one for your waist and to get those legs stretching and see just how balanced you are. Make sure your bottom stays in the saddle. Hands out level with your shoulders, then reach alternately right hand to right toe, up, then left hand to left toe. See if you can keep your back straight

Ankle gripping

Do this one leg at a time – and remember to sit up straight! It is great for loosening the muscle at the front of your thigh. Look ahead, grasp your ankle and draw your foot back and up.

Touching the ears/tail

Keeping your legs directly under you, lean slowly forwards to touch your pony's poll (between his ears). Now sit upright again then carefully turn to touch his quarters.

Leaning back

Face forwards, then lean back – slowly – until you are lying on your pony's back. Now sit up again. Try to keep your legs in the correct position all the time.

ONCE you are feeling secure and confident in trot, you are ready to try a canter. This is where things get really exciting! Canter is a rhythmic, rocking pace with three beats, which you will be able to clearly hear and feel.

Take a look at the sequence of pictures below. The first beat is made as one hind leg comes down. The second comes from the diagonal pair of the other hind and its opposite foreleg landing together. The final beat is from the other foreleg – this is called the leading leg. Then there is a brief moment of suspension when all four feet are off the ground, before the sequence starts again.

CANTER needs quite a bit of extra energy, and getting from trot into canter is a transition that many riders find difficult at first. Usually this is because they have not managed to get their pony trotting actively enough before they ask him to canter, so he quite simply has not got that extra 'oomph' that he needs. Or sometimes, the rider is trying so hard to urge her pony on, she slips out of position and the pony gets confused and unbalanced.

Transition: from trot to canter

1 Prepare to canter by getting the most energetic, balanced trot you can. Shorten the reins and tighten your bottom and leg muscles so he knows something is about to happen.

2 Sit to the trot. Now, staying as upright as you can and keeping a good contact on the pony's mouth, nudge with your inside leg on the girth, at the same time moving your outside leg slightly behind the girth.

3 The pony's first step of canter is called the strike off. You will know when this happens because it feels like a little bound forward. Keep your contact constant, but allow your hands to move with the pony's head. Although ponies usually enjoy cantering, some can be pretty hard to persuade to move up a gear. Be organised and determined. Sit up with your reins short enough. Get some bounce in that trot! Plan where you are going to ask (going into a corner is best) and use a firm nudge with your inside heel – staying upright. Be ready to use your whip just behind your inside leg if the pony does not respond straight away.

The canter

TIP

If your pony does not canter when you ask, don't let him just carry on trotting faster and faster. Get yourself together and settle back down to a good, active trot. Now, try again.

TIP

UNTIL you are more experienced, it is always best to ask for your canter coming into a corner or bend, or on a large circle. This helps your pony to keep himself in balance and encourages him to 'strike off' on to the correct leading leg.

FORGET IT! This rider will be exhausted before her pony gets the message to canter. Loopy reins, weight tipped forwards so the pony is all on his front end – they are far too unbalanced to manage a canter strike-off.

WHOA! The rider is so tense and hanging on so tightly that this pony will just keep trotting faster and never actually canter. She needs to lower and ease off her reins, bring her lower legs back, settle into a steady, relaxed trot and ask again.

Think about your position

The Canter

AS your pony starts to canter, think about staying sitting as straight as you can with your bottom right down in the saddle. Imagine your jodhpurs are stuck there with glue, and all the to-and-fro rocking of the canter is being absorbed by your hips going backwards and forwards with the movement. Of course they can only do this if your body is relaxed, so you must try not to stiffen up.

Your hands stay level and with a good contact. Don't hang on to the reins for dear life or your pony will wonder whether you really want canter or whether you want him to go back down to trot again. Relax your arms and wrists and let your hands follow the movement of the pony's head, keeping an even contact all the time.

Keep your legs directly underneath you, snug around the pony's sides but not clinging on. From here they are in a good position to give an extra leg aid if you sense your pony is thinking about falling back into trot before you want him to. Your legs must be relaxed too, to stop your knees tensing and your heels creeping up.

THE world seems to pass by you much faster in canter than in trot, so you do have to think quickly about where you are going and what you are doing. But the good news is that it is a much smoother movement, rather like sitting on a rocking-horse. The extra speed may make you tense up and bounce around in the saddle at first. But, as you learn to relax and keep upright, you will be able to sit into the saddle throughout the movement and really enjoy the feeling.

TIP

ALTHOUGH some ponies cannot wait to get into canter, quite a few need encouragement to make it and to keep going. This is especially true if they are not particularly well-balanced, are in a small arena or are lazy characters. Don't try and urge a slow pony on by leaning forward like a jockey (above). You have the best chance of keeping a good canter all the way around the school if you keep your shoulders back, sit deep and keep a good contact on the reins. If you feel the pony slowing – perhaps going into a corner – give him an extra nudge with your inside heel. That's better (right)!

OKAY, so you are going a whole lot faster in canter than trot, but that is no excuse for riding like a Grand Prix driver or motor-biking the corners. Steady your pony by sitting right up and squeezing the reins a little, especially the outside rein, as you approach a corner. Use lots of inside leg. If you let your pony hurtle round he will get totally out of balance and may slip.

2

IF you are cantering on a circle or around a bend (left), you use just the same aids for turning as in any pace. Your inside hand asks for the pony to look around the bend and your inside leg asks him to keep the energy up and bend his body. Your outside hand allows a little so he can look slightly to the inside, and your outside leg stays just behind the girth to stop him swinging his back end out.

OOPS! This (right) is what happens if you tense your leg and grip up with your knees. If you lose a stirrup it is best to come down to trot and start again.

It's not surprising this pony is hardly cantering when the reins are so long. If the rider gathers him together much more, and uses her legs, she will get lots more 'omph'!

TIP

AIM for a canter with short, bouncy strides in a nice one-two-three rhythm. This will keep your pony balanced and give you good control. To get a bouncier canter, nudge your pony on with your inside heel in time with each stride. But make sure your reins are nice and short, or he will only go faster and get more disorganised.

From canter to trot

WHEN you want to slow down from canter to trot, check you are sitting tall. Stop sending your pony on with your legs, but still keep them close to his sides directly under your body. Brace your back and press down with your bottom into the saddle. Put pressure on the reins until you feel him slow and break into trot, then ease it off (but keep your contact). Remember to sit for a few beats of the trot after your transition to help you get yourself organised.

Make your transition as smooth as possible. Try not to let yourself – and your pony – just fall out of canter into a heap, losing all your 'go' at once. As you make the downward transition, keep sitting up and sending him on so he does not think he has finished work for the day!

SO what is all this you have heard about getting the 'right leg' in canter? Well, though you may think this is rather technical to be bothered with when you are only just learning to canter, it is important. Because, unless your pony is cantering on the correct 'leading leg' whenever he is going around the arena or on a circle, he will never be balanced. He will feel less comfortable and may even trip over.

Sequence

You will remember that the three-beat sequence of the canter footfalls ends with one foreleg coming down. It is easy to see why it is called the leading leg, because if you glance down while the pony is cantering you can see it stretch forwards.

Listening to the hoof-beats, you can hear the pony's emphasis on the leading leg – *duh, duh, DUH*. This leg takes all his weight by itself as it pushes him forwards to the next stride.

If you are cantering along in a straight line, say out in the field on a hack, it does not really matter which of the forelegs is the leading leg. But if you are in an arena or cantering a circle, the leading leg must be the pony's inside foreleg. So, if you are on the right rein the correct leg is the right foreleg, and on the left rein, it is the left one.

Listen out for the hoof beats

AS soon as you are cantering, glance down quickly (don't lean!) to check if you are on the correct leg – you will see the leading leg stretching forwards with each stride.

After a while you will learn to tell just by the feel, especially as being on the wrong leg does actually feel less

comfortable. If you spot you are wrong, come back down to trot immediately and get ready to try again. You will not be able to get your pony to change leading legs while he is still cantering along – that is, until you are a dressage or showjumping star!

Canter 3

Getting the right leg

HOW can you make sure your pony strikes off so he goes on to the correct leading leg?

1. MAKE A GOOD TRANSITION
Practise your transitions so your pony is prepared with a good, active trot and he responds to your aids to canter immediately without getting unbalanced.

2. ALWAYS ASK FOR CANTER IN A CORNER OR ON A CIRCLE (right). As long as he is in balance coming into the bend, this will mean the easiest thing for him to do is begin his canter stride with his outside hind leg – meaning the inside fore will correctly become his leading leg.

3. BEND HIS HEAD AND NECK slightly to the inside as you ask. This is hard to remember at first when there is so much to think about, but as you improve, try it. Flexing the pony to the inside of the curve by squeezing your inside rein as you give the canter aids helps him understand which 'bend' and which leg you want.

QUICK QUIZ

Can you tell which of these horses is cantering on the correct leg?

ANSWER: A

YOU will be looking forward to learning how to jump with excitement and maybe a few jitters, wondering whether you are going to be able to make your pony go over the fence – and whether you will land in the same place as he does on the other side!

Jumping is a thrilling part of riding and tackling small fences is nowhere near as difficult as it looks, as long as, by now, you have got a secure position in the saddle and feel confident and in control of your pony at walk, trot and canter.

Jumping, like everything else in riding, is about balance, and, again, you cannot expect to get it right straight away, or to get it right every time. When you first start, expect to have quite a few jerky jumps and maybe some sticky moments. You might even fall off

Jumping

a few times, though, hopefully, you will slither to the ground and land on your feet without any damage being done. Soon, with the help of your instructor and an experienced pony, and starting off over poles on the ground and very low, simple obstacles, you will build your confidence and get the knack of sticking with the motion. Then you will really start enjoying it.

1 The Approach

This is very important. A pony that approaches the fence with plenty of 'oomph', going straight and in balance, will find it easy to carry on and jump. All you have to worry about is staying steady and letting him get on with it. But a bad approach makes life difficult and gives him plenty of excuses for saying 'No thanks' or jumping awkwardly. For small jumps, approach either in trot or in canter. Sit as still as you can, but keep your pony going forwards in a straight line towards the centre of the jump. Be ready to urge him on if you feel him slowing down.

2 The Take-off

In the last stride before the jump, the pony steadies as he weighs it up. He brings his hind legs underneath and pushes off, lifting up his front legs. He takes off around the same distance from the fence as it is high. There' s no need for you to tell your pony when to take off – as long as he is going forwards in balance he will decide this for himself. He may want to get close to have a good look first. If so, keep your body still but use your legs more strongly. Concentrate on trying to stay in synch with him when he takes off. Always look up, this will keep your body straight. The movement will swing your body forwards, so let your hands go forward so the pony can stretch his neck out without getting his mouth pulled. Don't lean forward over his neck too early, or you will make it hard to take off.

3 The Moment of Suspension

This is when you are in the air. Over low jumps all four legs are only off the ground together for an instant, but as you get on to bigger jumps you will feel several seconds as the pony goes over. During this time you need to be squatting in jumping position close to the pony, and as in balance with him as you can. Your weight is off his back and your legs directly underneath you (see next page for more about the jumping position). As the neck stretches out, allow with your hands by letting your arms reach forwards.

4 Landing

The horse comes down on one of his forelegs first, followed quickly by the other. As this happens, his head and neck come up. This bit feels bumpy to the rider, and it is easy to get pulled forward or thrown off balance. So keep your lower leg well under you or push it slightly forwards. Avoid collapsing onto your pony's neck or leaning your hands on him.

How a pony jumps

WHEN a pony jumps, all he is actually doing is taking an extra-large canter stride, with added 'pop' in it, in order to clear whatever it is that is in his way. So if you have got the hang of canter, you will soon get the feel of jumping small fences. Of course, when it comes to top-class showjumping, that extra-big stride is huge. But even so, it's basically the same action as the one a pony uses when he is just going over a small cross-pole.

5 Recovery

This is the first stride taken after landing. Now you can gently sit back down into the saddle and take up more contact with the reins again. Use your legs to keep your pony moving forwards. As quickly as you can, get organised, because, as you improve, there could be another fence coming up!

NO-ONE is expecting you to jump over big fences right away, or instantly be able to sit perfectly throughout the jump. Learning to stay with the pony's movement takes quite a bit of skill and many practice jumps!

Getting into the right position over the jump is crucial, because it helps you stay secure and, not interfering with the pony, gives him the best chance to clear the fence smoothly and without knocking it. A good jumping position also makes

Jumping 2

you look stylish and 'together' with your pony – and means that you can see where you are heading! Before you start to jump, always:

Check your girth is tight – or you could end up on

the floor before you even reach the jumps!

Shorten your stirrups – stirrups are always raised a few holes for jumping, because this makes it easier to get into and hold the jumping position.

YOU can practise jumping position both standing on the ground or on a pony that is standing still. Remember, you should be able to balance perfectly with your feet flat on the ground, or in the stirrups, without toppling forwards or backwards.

■ Look up and ahead, between the pony's ears.

■ Try to flatten your back, sticking your bottom out and your chest down towards the pony's neck, so you are hovering just above the saddle seat. Think of your body and legs as a big 'W' on its end. What you are aiming to do is to squash up the W as much as you can, so all the angles are closed up.

■ Keep your lower leg right underneath you. Let all your weight sink down through your heels.

Practising jumping position

■ Don't rest your hands on the pony's neck. When you are balanced, you will be able to move them forwards or backwards quite easily.

■ Now practise keeping your balance in jumping position when your pony is on the move.

Don't get into a bad position...

YOU can see from these photos why it is worth perfecting your jumping position, especially as you go on to tackle bigger jumps. All of these ponies are finding it hard to do a nice, rounded jump because their riders are not sitting correctly. Imagine all of the photos with the pony taken out – none of these riders would be able to stay in balance on their own two feet, would they?

Standing in the stirrups

STANDING in the stirrups (right) is another common fault. This rider is trying to jump the fence for the pony. He has gone out of the saddle too far and too soon, instead of waiting for the pony to come up towards him. Rather than squashing down into jumping position, he is just standing up, with straight legs. If this pony had decided to refuse, or else stumbled on landing, he would be too far forwards out of balance and would fall off.

Getting left behind

GETTING 'left behind' is one of the most common problems and does not only happen when you are learning. Instead of going with the pony's forward movement as he takes off, the rider is too far back and gets jolted out of the saddle as the pony's hind legs come up. If this happens, try to slip the reins through your fingers so you don't jab the pony in the mouth. Make sure you are poised in a balanced, slightly forward position as you approach, then squash down into jumping position as you feel the pony coming up as he takes off.

Looking and leaning down

THIS rider (above) is well squashed down, but with all her weight flung to one side she is making her pony 'flatten' over the jump. Look how his ear is back, thinking 'What's she doing?' The chances are he will veer to one side over the fence, or knock it down, and he may well tip her over his shoulder as he lands!

OUCH! (above). Always try and allow with your hands as the pony's neck stretches forwards, or jumping will not be a very easy or enjoyable experience for him.

THERE are several kinds of exercises that your instructor will use to help improve your jumping technique. Even the very best, most experienced riders use these in their schooling, especially when teaching a young horse or pony to jump.

Jumping 3

Using Trotting Poles . . .

ONE of the best exercises for ponies and riders is to use a line of poles on the ground, often called 'trotting poles'. From the pony's point of view, this teaches him to be co-ordinated, to pick up his feet and get in a nice rhythm. Novice riders can learn to get their balance over the poles before trying a 'real' jump, and start feeling what kind of regular tempo the pony needs to be going in for jumping.

The poles are laid on the ground either singly, or in a line with a set distance in between. You can tackle them in walk at first and then, when you feel secure and well in control, try the exercise in trot. Your instructor will make sure the poles are always the right distance apart so your pony should not trip over them. For ponies, this is 1.2-1.3m (4ft - 4ft 6 ins), for horses slightly longer.

ALWAYS approach in a straight line, aiming for the centre of the poles. Take your weight slightly off the saddle as you approach, though you do not need to fold down into full jumping position. Remember to look ahead, keep a good contact on the reins and use your legs to keep asking the pony to go forwards.

TRY to stay in a good position over the poles. You may feel the pony slowing up, so squeeze him on with your legs, trying not to lose your balance as you do this. You will feel the bounce-bounce-bounce as your pony picks his feet up higher. It will jolt, so this is when you need to try to absorb the movement in your ankles, knees and hips – a bit like you do in rising trot, but instead of going up and down in the saddle, you are hovering in balance just over it.

This rider's pony (below left) is trotting on nicely through the poles, though her weight could be a little more forwards with her bottom just out of the saddle.

YOU will probably feel the pony wanting to stretch his neck out a bit more than in ordinary trot, so let him do this by allowing your hands forwards. Do not fall onto his neck though or give the reins away, because you need them to help him stay balanced. If you feel yourself getting unsteady, don't snatch at the reins and hurt the pony's mouth. Grab the neckstrap or a chunk of mane.

ONCE you are feeling organised over trotting poles, it's time for some real jumping. Your instructor will probably first add a small jump – such as a cross-pole – to the end of the line of poles on the ground. The good thing about this is that the poles leading up to the jump make sure your pony is in exactly the right spot to take off when he gets there, so you don't have to worry about that. All you need to concentrate on is keeping a balanced position over the poles, looking up and encouraging your pony to stay in an active, forward-going rhythm all the way. Remember not to go right forwards before your pony actually takes off, and to allow a little with your hands as he goes over. Don't let him waver to the side – head straight for the centre of the jump.

Starting Grid Work

THE exercise on this page – poles leading to a single jump – is a very simple form of grid. Grid-work is any jumping exercise involving different combinations of poles on the ground and low jumps set out in a line. It is very good for ponies and riders because it helps you practise keeping your position and rhythm through the line. It is fun and confidence-boosting for everyone, because the poles and jumps are arranged at set distances to place the pony exactly right as he goes along, so it is easy for him to keep going onwards and easy for you to stay in balance with him.

The rider is using her legs to encourage her pony through the poles to the first cross-pole of the grid. See how she is looking ahead where she is going

The rider could fold forward a bit more to allow her pony a little more rein over the first fence.

Her pony lands in canter and is keen to carry on through the grid. Now the rider sits up with a good contact, to help re-balance him over the next pole.

The final fence in this grid is a small spread. The pony jumps out well, but would have appreciated some more freedom to stretch his neck by his rider bringing her hands forward instead of resting them on his crest.

POLES on the ground in front of a jump make things simpler for a rider, because they put the pony on just the right stride to take off in a good place in front of the jump. As you get better, you will have to learn how to tackle a jump on its own, without a 'placing pole' in front.

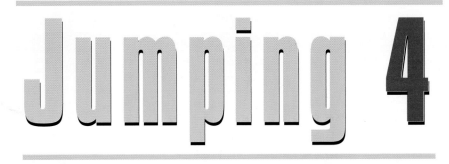

Jumping 4

TIP

ALWAYS come round in a wide circle or arc towards a line of poles or a fence, to help keep your pony balanced. Otherwise he either will not have enough 'Go', or, will start to rush

Tackling Bigger Fences

It is important that as you approach the fence your pony is:

Going actively forwards: (picture, above). You need a bouncy but controlled trot or canter.

Going straight: Come around in a wide arc, looking towards the fence. Then head towards the fence in a straight line, aiming for the centre.

Looking up: Eyes up over the fence, not down!

Sitting still and in balance: Keep your legs on to encourage the pony forwards, but otherwise try to keep as still as you can. Nothing puts a pony off the idea of jumping quicker than a rider who keeps shifting around or pulling him in the mouth as he approaches the fence.

TIP

IF you are approaching in canter, make sure you are on the correct leading leg before coming round towards the jump. It will help the pony get a balanced approach. Look where you are going, as it helps you to plan a good route and turns your body slightly, too.

Positive Thinking

MOST ponies enjoy jumping as long as their rider makes it easy and comfortable for them. Some can be lazy or uncooperative, and following another more willing pony will usually encourage a reluctant jumper. Most of all though, whether a pony will jump or not is down to you.

Always be positive and determined about jumping, even when the fences are only low. If you are not sure, your pony will sense this and the chances are he will decide not to bother himself! As you approach a line of poles or a fence, think not just about your position but about getting your pony really moving on purposefully.

We are not talking about going fast – just with plenty of bounce and energy (called impulsion). So that means lots of leg and a good feel on the reins, not leaving them flapping loose for the pony to choose his own speed or run out to one side. Be determined you are going to get over that jump, and ready to use more leg or give a quick smack with the whip if you suspect your pony is having second thoughts.

Making the wrong approach

PRESENTING a pony badly at a fence, by having a disorganised approach, is bad news.

If by the time you reach the jump your pony is out of control, doing his own thing completely, or totally off balance, the result is almost guaranteed to be either a refusal or a run-out to the side.

Even if he is willing to take off, the chances are the pony will probably jump awkwardly and knock the fence down.

As you become more experienced and confident, your instructor will soon have you following one fence with another. Before you know it you will be doing a series of jumps to make up a course.

Jumping 5

Tackling more than one fence

WHEN one jump comes after another you need to really have your wits about you and think ahead so you can give your pony good preparation for every one, not just the first! As soon as you land over one fence you need to recover quickly, organise yourself again and set your pony up for the next one – remembering all the points we mentioned for a good approach. If you tackle each fence as it comes, before you know it you will have finished – with a clear round!

Upright to start

THERE are lots of different styles of fence, but all belong to two basic types. The first type you will start off jumping is called an upright (pictured below). Uprights are fixed up on a single set of jump stands or 'wings'. They have no depth, just height, which the pony jumps up and over.

Taking on spreads

AS you progress, you will start jumping spreads, too. A spread fence has some depth to it, so the pony must not only jump up, but stretch out as well, to clear it. It is usually built on two sets of jump stands or wings, one directly behind the other.

At the double

TWO fences set quite close together are called a 'double'. They are always placed the right distance apart so your pony should take either one or two strides between them. When you progress to jumping a course that includes a double, you will learn how to pace out the distance on foot to check how many strides there are between each fence (called each 'element'). With practice you will soon be flying high with your pony. You may get the chance to show off your skills at a show (right).

Picking

I F you thought that canter was fast and exciting, you will love the buzz of galloping. Gallop is the horse's fastest pace, the one you see racehorses using as they thunder round the track.

Your pony will not travel at quite that speed, but he still moves pretty quickly in gallop, so you must feel safe and secure in canter before you ask him to move on any faster. Also you need to be sure your 'brakes' are working and that you stay in balance and control all the time.

Choosing a location

There is not enough room to gallop in an arena, so you will only be able to try it out on a hack. Even so, do not try a gallop any old where. Choose a place where the ground is level and firm and where you know you

Transition: Canter to gallop

WHEN you go from canter to gallop, you will not feel a sudden change of pace or tempo as you do with the other upward transitions. Once you feel you have a good canter, just ease the reins a little, use your legs more and come forward slightly with your weight out of the saddle, as if you were in jumping position. Now you will feel your pony start to pick up more speed. Listen for his hoofbeats. When the 1-2-3 footfalls of canter turn to a faster 1-2-3-4, and your pony seems to be stretching out to take longer strides, then you know you are galloping.

... and from gallop to canter

WHEN you want to slow down, sit back down in the saddle. With your legs well underneath you, put pressure on the reins then release it, then feel on the reins again and release them. Use this 'give and take' action to slow the pony. If you just pull continuously, if he is keen to keep going he will take hold of the bit in his mouth and pull back against you.

up speed

The buzz of the gallop!

will be able to stop the pony safely. Remember that ponies cantering together often get excited and start racing, so it is best to practise your first gallops on your own.

In gallop, if you were to stay sitting down in the saddle as you do when cantering, it would be hard work for the pony. This is because his whole centre of balance shifts forwards when he is galloping.

Keeping balanced

Your aim is always to stay right over your pony's centre of balance. Taking up a more forward seat allows him to stay balanced and use his hindquarters to go faster.

It is best to shorten up your stirrups beforehand, which helps you get into a steady forward position more easily. Keeping your reins short so you can feel the pony's mouth,

bring your upper body towards his neck as for jumping. Your lower legs want to stay directly under you, with all your weight pushing down through the heels. Concertina-ed up, your legs and body can absorb the movement.

Don't forget to look up!

Staying forwards

Look (below and far left) how the pony's 'outline' lengthens in gallop as he stretches out to reach top speed.

Staying forwards helps him use his hindquarters and stay in balance.

Pick somewhere safe and level to gallop, and try the feel out on your own before you pick up speed with others around.

If you feel your pony getting too keen, sit up and steady him right away.

WITH a bit of luck, you will have an instructor who makes learning to ride real fun and thinks of lots of ways of brightening up your lessons with games and other exercises that gives everyone a laugh and improves your riding skills at the same time.

Perhaps you have seen mounted games at a show or gymkhana? They are really just party games on horseback.

Games are great for your balance and confidence, and ponies love them, too. If your instructor has not already thought of it, you could ask if you could do some at the end of a lesson. Or, if you have a pony of your own, get together with a few friends for some gymkhana action!

TIP

BY all means have a good time, but never get carried away and start being rough with your pony. If your pony is lagging behind, don't flap about and hassle him, but think about your riding and how to get him moving along more speedily. Be careful not to yank on the reins. Your voice can get the pony's attention, but don't shout!

Ways to play

1 Egg & Spoon

THIS is similar to the sack race, except that you collect an egg and spoon and have to carry the egg back to the finish – leading your pony at the same time! If you drop the egg, you have to pick it up before you can carry on.

TIP DON'T drag your pony along behind you or let him rush off ahead, or you are sure to drop the egg. Try to run alongside the pony's shoulder.

2 Flag race

(Picture, left) Ride as fast as you can to the end of the arena and pick up a flag from the holder there. Now, whizz back to the other end and put it – carefully – into the holder there. Repeat this until all the flags have been collected and safely delivered, then zoom across the finish line.

TIP CHECK your speed as you approach the containers, or you will find that you over-shoot or cannot get the flag in. It is easier if you lean right down.

Games

3 Potato race

RACE to the end of the arena, dismount, pick up a potato, get back on and whizz back again, putting the potato into a bucket at the other end. Ride around the bucket and carry on until you have transferred all the potatoes, one at a time. If you drop a potato, you will need to dismount and pick it up.

TIP WAIT until you are right alongside the bucket, then lean right down to put the potato in rather than dropping it, or it might bounce straight out again!

4 Sack race

JUST like the sack race on school sports day. Ride to the end of the arena, dismount, clamber into the sack and make for home as fast as you can. Sometimes the pony is left for someone else to hold, but older riders can try leading the pony as they go.

5 Bending race

HERE you have to weave your way in and out down a line of poles or markers and back again to the start. The first pony and rider home win, but they must not have knocked over any markers or missed any out.

TIP KEEP as close to the poles as you can to save time, and, at the end of the line, make a tight turn rather than going half a mile further than you need to!

6 Chase Me Charlie

THIS is not actually a race, but it is still a popular gymkhana game for more experienced riders. Riders follow each other over two small fences, one on each side of the arena. If you knock one down or your pony refuses, you are out.

After everyone has had a go, both fences are raised one hole for the next round. The rider who jumps clear over the highest fence wins. There is another form of this game called 'Follow Me Fred', where each round the fence gets narrower and narrower!

TIP HOLD the sack right up above your knees and look up, and you will be less likely to trip over. Practise getting into that sack lightning fast!

TIP REMEMBER all you have learnt about a good approach to each jump, to help your pony jump clear. Don't crowd up to the rider in front, or your pony will not see the jump in time.

NOW that you have mastered the basics of controlling your pony at all paces, you can begin to enjoy yourself taking him into the countryside – 'hacking'. The first hacks you go on will probably be with your instructor in a small group. Even later on, if you have a pony of your own, it is best to ride with a friend or two rather than on your own, for safety's sake.

You can explore in all kinds of places that cars cannot go, and hacking out can be loads of fun. You will find it different from riding in the manege in many ways: your pony is much livelier and more responsive. And you never know quite what is going to happen – a bird might fly out of a hedge and startle him, for instance. So you have to be ready to anticipate possible problems or react quickly if your pony makes an unexpected move. If your pony does start to get excited or fidgety riding out in a group, try to relax and calm him down. Slow to a walk and ask the other riders not to crowd in close. Always keep a safe distance between ponies, wherever you are riding.

BEFORE YOU GO ...

- Tell someone where you are heading and when you expect to be back.
- Take a coin for a phone call (or a mobile phone!).
- If it is going to be quite a long ride, it is worth taking a small saddle bag or rucksack with a first-aid kit, hoof pick, length of baler twine for emergency tack repairs, spare rein and stirrup leather and reflective gear.
- Wear the right clothing for the weather conditions.
- Check the weather before you go. It is not a bright idea to set out as the light is fading or in poor weather.

Opening and closing gates

GATES are often too heavy or stiff to be opened from the back of a pony, in which case you will need to get off. But it is still handy to know how to get through without dismounting. Here's how:

1 Walk up to the gate quietly and position your pony alongside it so you can easily reach down to the latch. Take both reins into one hand, keeping them short. Undo the latch and push the gate away from you.

2 If you can, keep a hold of it as you walk forwards, pushing it as you go. Then use your inside leg behind the girth to ask the pony to move his hindquarters around but keep his forelegs still. If you cannot hold on to the gate, make sure the gap is wide enough before you move through, and that it is not going to swing back on you.

3 Now your pony should be positioned facing or alongside the gate the other side, with you holding it. Ask him to walk slowly forwards to push it shut. If you end up letting go, see the gate does not bang and swing back out again into your pony. Always fasten gates properly before riding away.

About

Crossing water

You might encounter a stream out on your hack that needs to be crossed. Some ponies are nervous of water and need encouragement to step in, but many love a splash. In fact, some love it so much they fancy getting down to roll, so if your pony starts to paw at the water, urge him forwards quickly! Never ride into a deep or fast-flowing river.

In the woods

THERE are a few hazards to watch out for when you are riding in woodland. Rabbit holes could trap a pony's foot, and fallen logs on the ground could make him stumble.

So always check the ground ahead before trotting or cantering. Low branches are another hazard – so be ready to duck! If you come across a log that seems like it could be jumped, look before you leap. Go to the other side to make sure the landing is safe first.

Uphill task

When riding up a hill or incline, lean forwards, like this, with your weight slightly out of the saddle to help your

pony use his hindquarters freely. Look up and don't let your legs slip back. Allow your hands forwards, but keep a light contact on the reins.

All downhill

On downhill stretches you can help your pony to balance himself by leaning slightly backwards. Don't lean right back unless the drop is very steep. Give your pony a little rein, but don't let the reins sag.

COUNTRY CODE

BEFORE riding out in the countryside, learn the rider's Country Code and always respect its rules:

● Keep to official bridleways and public riding tracks (riders are not allowed on footpaths).

● Close all gates behind you.

● Never leave litter.

● Stay in walk through fields with livestock in and keep to the edge.

● Never light fires.

Cross

IF you have watched the riders tackling those enormous fences at three-day events like Badminton, then you probably can't wait to have a go at some cross-country jumping! It may take many many years of training before a horse and rider can face mind-boggling obstacles like that. But, if you enjoy jumping and are confident about it, then you will get a real thrill from even some simple cross-country fences. Unlike show-jumps, which are usually made of brightly-painted poles and fillers, cross-country jumps are all 'natural' obstacles such as logs or walls, or else rustic fences made of natural materials like timber or brush. The other difference is that cross-country fences are solid and fixed – they don't knock

BECAUSE you are riding a cross-country course outdoors, you can bowl on at a faster canter than you normally would when show-jumping in an arena. Between the fences take up a forward position off the pony's back, as for galloping (see page 52). But as you come towards a fence, sit more upright again and steady your pony to balance and prepare him. Although when you are doing cross-country you need to get your pony going in quite a fast, energetic canter, never let him dash headlong at a fence, however keen he is. Steady before each obstacle, to give the pony a chance to see what is coming up.

Cross country kit

YOU will both need some extra kit for cross-country:

Body protector: Maybe you already wear a body protector for all your riding. If you don't generally wear one, you will need one for cross-country, to save too many bumps and bruises if you do hit the deck!

Gloves: Make sure you are wearing gloves, as your pony may pull or the reins may get slippy with sweat.

Surcingle: Fasten an extra girth called a 'surcingle' over and around the saddle.

Boots: Protect your pony's legs from knocks with brushing boots. Many riders wear bright jumpers and matching silks on their helmets for cross-country competitions.

country

down. So that means that although you will be approaching your fences faster than in showjumping, you have to be just as careful. If your pony did hit something, it would not be the fence that fell down!

Be confident to make your pony brave

HERE are some riders tackling different types of cross-country fences.

Always ride on determinedly as you approach each one, especially 'spooky' fences such as shiny barrels, or the water. If you are confident, you will make your pony brave. Sit well back as your pony lands if a fence is lower on the far side than it is on the take-off side, or you are going down some 'steps'. When a horse cannot see what is on the other side of the fence he needs to have lots of trust and confidence in his rider.

RIDERS can compete across natural fences at 'cross-country events' or 'hunter trials'. A cross-country course is also one of the three phases of a horse trial, one-day event or – for the real experts – a three-day event (below). The other phases are dressage and showjumping.

T would be great if we could ride straight out of the yard on to a track or bridleway without having to worry about dodging the traffic on the roads. But, unfortunately, most of us will have to ride on the road sometimes.

Many drivers are considerate to riders, but you will always come across some who fail to understand that a pony is an animal and needs to be passed slowly and with great care.

So, before you venture out on to the road, you need to be in full control of your pony. If possible, go with an older person at first. Never risk taking an inexperienced pony on the road on your own, or one who is nervous of traffic or likely to misbehave, as this could be very dangerous.

You will need to be extra-alert, looking and listening for what is coming up in front or behind, and be ready for anything that might possibly make your pony shy. You also need to swot up on some of the rules of the road that apply to riders, and learn how to give hand signals to tell motorists what you are intending to do.

Using hand signals

ALWAYS make your hand signals clear and obvious :

TURNING As you approach the turn, check for traffic in front and behind. Hold your arm out straight, level with your shoulder. Keep looking and listening. Do not make a turn to the right unless the road is completely clear. If necessary, stop to wait, then signal again before crossing. Never move to the centre and stop there.

STOP, PLEASE There may be times when you need to ask other road users to stop behind you rather than try to go past. Look behind, and turning your body slightly in the saddle so you can see behind you, bend your elbow and hold your right hand up.

SLOW DOWN PLEASE If you want a driver who is approaching to slow down a bit, hold your right arm straight out with the palm down. Move it slowly up and down.

THANKS Whenever a motorist slows down to pass, or waits for you, always thank them. Then they will be just as considerate next time they meet a rider on the road.

safety

1 RIDE close to the verge, going in the same direction as the traffic. NEVER ride or stop in the centre of the road.

2 ONLY ride two-abreast if the road is wide. At other times ride in single file. If you are in a group it is safest to have the most experienced riders and steadiest ponies at the front and rear of the line. If you are out with friends, remember this is not the time to be dawdling along and chatting!

Rules of the road

3 YOU can walk or trot steadily on the road, but you must NEVER canter or gallop.

4 DO NOT ride on the pavement in a built-up area, or on any grass verges that have been mown.

5 WHEN you want to turn or move out around a parked car, use your hand signal well in advance. Keep looking and listening.

Riding at dusk

IT is best not to ride at night, because your pony cannot be seen by other road users. When you must, kit yourself and your pony up with reflective gear, which reflects car headlights. Get a fluorescent reflective tabard or cross-belt and your pony should wear some reflective leg bands. Remember – be seen and be safe!

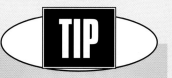

TIP

EVEN the most sensible of ponies might 'spook'. Be ready so you can react quickly, straightening your pony up and getting back in position close to the verge. Don't hang on to the reins too tightly. Always carry your whip in your right hand (the one nearest traffic).

ACTION: The way a pony moves.

AIDS: Signals given by the rider to communicate with the pony.

BALANCE: The way the pony and rider's weight are spread.

BEND: The curve through the pony's body as he is moving around a corner or on a circle.

BIT: The piece of the bridle that is held in the pony's mouth, usually made of

Get to know your inside and outside reins *(above)*. The inside rein is towards the centre of the arena, or the inside of the circle you are riding.

metal. The reins are attached to the bit and are the rider's means of giving hand aids to the pony.

BOMBPROOF: Used to describe a pony that is especially safe and sensible.

BOUNCE FENCE: A pair of showjumps placed at a certain distance quite close to each other, so that the pony will jump the first and then the second without needing to take a canter stride in between.

BUCK: When a disobedient pony puts his head down and arches his back, with a jump in the air.

CANTLE: The back of the saddle.

CAVALETTI: An old-fashioned type of small schooling fence which uses a pole fixed at each end to a X-shaped stand.

CENTRE LINE: An imaginary line down the centre of the school from end to end, passing through X.

CHANGING THE REIN: Going around the school or arena in the opposite direction to the one you were travelling in before.

CLEAR ROUND: Completing a course of jumps without collecting any penalties.

CONTACT: The link between the pony's mouth and the reins. Often described as your 'feel' on the reins, or by the amount of 'weight' in the reins.

CROSS-POLE: A small jump made using two poles set in an X, so one end of each is supported on the jump stand, with the other resting on the ground.

DIAGONAL: (1) An imaginary line crossing the schooling arena from one of the corner markers to another corner marker on the far side, passing through X. (2) The pairs of legs used by the pony as he trots and which the rider must learn to recognise, so she is sitting to the correct pair.

DISMOUNT: To get off the pony.

DRESSAGE: Training a horse or pony to make him more supple and obedient.

DOUBLE: Two show jumps set close together, that are classed as one obstacle with two parts or 'elements'. A double can have one or two strides of canter between each element, or be a bounce.

FIGURE OF EIGHT: School movement that is the shape of a number 8.

FILLER: A large board used instead of more poles to 'fill in' a show jump, underneath the top pole.

FOREHAND: The front half of the pony, in front of the saddle.

FORWARD SEAT: When the rider positions herself with her weight balanced just out of the saddle, slightly forwards. Used for cantering cross-country, galloping and jumping.

GIRTH: Wide strap that holds the saddle in place, under the pony's belly.

GRID: Sequence of poles on the ground and small fences used for training the pony and rider for jumping.

HINDQUARTERS: The back half of the pony, behind the saddle.

IMPULSION: Energy and 'bounce' created by the pony's hindquarters as he moves along.

INSIDE HAND/LEG: The hand or leg on the side of the pony nearest to the inside when you are riding in an arena or on a circle.

LEADING FILE: The rider at the front of a group going in single file.

LEADING LEG: The leg of the pony that reaches furthest forward in canter, completing the stride. In canter to the left, the correct leading leg is the near

(left) fore. In canter to the right, it is the off (right) fore.

LEG UP: A way of mounting where someone else helps lift you on.

LUNGEING: Training the pony or rider by using a long rein to control the pony, which moves in a circle around the handler or instructor.

MANEGE: An enclosed arena used for training and exercising. The surface may be grass, sand or be made of a synthetic all-weather material, but it should always be level.

MOUNTING BLOCK: A safe step where you can stand to help you mount.

NAPPING: When a naughty pony ignores his rider and refuses to go forwards.

NEAR SIDE: The left-hand side of the pony.

NECKSTRAP: A long leather strap that goes around the pony's neck for a novice rider to hold on to for extra security. May be part of a martingale.

OFF SIDE: The right-hand side of the pony.

OUTSIDE HAND/LEG: The hand or leg on the outside when the pony is moving around an arena or on a circle.

POMMEL: The front of the saddle.

PULLER: A naughty pony that leans his weight on the bit and does not listen to the rider's rein aids.

REFUSAL: When a pony stops in front of a fence.

RUNNING UP THE STIRRUPS: Pushing the stirrup irons up the back of the leathers to the top and threading the spare leather through the iron. Neatens and secures the irons for leading the pony when the rider has dismounted.

RUN OUT: When the pony runs around the side of the fence instead of going over it.

SCHOOL MOVEMENTS: Exercises performed in an arena using set markers. Used in training horses and riders.

SEAT: The rider's position in the saddle. A good, independent seat does not rely on the reins or stirrups to stay secure and balanced.

SERPENTINE: A school movement taking up the whole length and width of the arena, shaped like a snake or 'S'.

SHYING: When a frightened or naughty pony moves quickly sideways.

SPREAD: A type of jump that has width as well as height, made using more than one set of jump stands or wings.

STRIKE OFF: The first step that a pony takes in canter.

SURCINGLE: A narrow, stretchy strap used over the saddle in cross-country competitions, for extra security.

SUSPENSION: When all the pony's legs are off the ground at the same time. There is a 'moment of suspension' in both trot and canter and also when the pony is over the top of a jump.

TRANSITION: When the pony changes pace. Can be upwards, eg. from walk to trot, or downwards, eg. from canter to trot.

TROTTING POLES: Long poles laid flat on the ground, often in a line. Used for teaching riders and ponies to jump.

TRACK: (1) The imaginary 'path' around the edge of an arena. The outside track is right on the edge and the inside track is just inside this. (2) The route taken around a course of showjumps.

UPRIGHT: A type of jump that has height but no extra width, made using just one set of jump stands or wings.

WINGS: Supports used to hold up poles or fillers to make showjumps. Can be made of wood or plastic.

Ride positively and you will give your pony confidence when tackling cross country fences.

Two more great H&P titles to collect

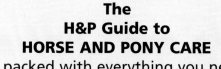